Napoleon's Travelling Bookshelf

Sarah Hesketh was born in 1983 and grew up in Pendle, East Lancashire. She attended Merton College, Oxford and holds an MA in Creative Writing from UEA. In 2007 her collaboration with composer Alastair Caplin was performed at the Leeds Lieder Festival. She currently works as Assistant Director at the writers' charity English PEN.

www.sarahhesketh.co.uk

Napoleon's Travelling Bookshelf

Sarah Hesketh

To Chris,
very many thanks
for coming. Hope you
enjoyed the enclosed,
Sarah
xxx.

Penned in the Margins
LONDON

PUBLISHED BY PENNED IN THE MARGINS
53 Arcadia Court, 45 Old Castle Street, London E1 7NY
www.pennedinthemargins.co.uk

First published 2009

Printed in Great Britain by the MPG Books Group, Bodmin and King's Lynn

ISBN
0-9553846-6-4
978-0-9553846-6-0

ACKNOWLEDGEMENTS

I would like to thank the editors of the following publications in which some of these poems, some in altered versions, have appeared: *Agenda, Cheque Enclosed, Gift: Spring, PEN International: The Writer Next Door, Stop Sharpening Your Knives (3), West Branch.*

~

Special thanks to my family – Mum, Rob, Grandma, Dad and Pam. To Tom Chivers for being patient. And to Benjamin Thompson for nagging.

Further thanks to Liz Adams, Stacy Anderson, Polly Clark, Julian Fielding and my fellow cube-dwellers at Cove Park, Katie Hays, Jonathan Heawood and the staff of English PEN, Derek Johns, Barbara and Richard Maycock, Bernard O'Donoghue, Denise Riley, Lora Stimson, George Szirtes and Anna Towers.

Commendations and a copy of the magazine to Alex Runchman and Cate Whetzel, Agi Lehózcky and Meghan Purvis, Stephanie Leal and Jennifer Thompson – fellow poets in arms.

CONTENTS

For mum.
Sorry - not that many happy poems.

Napoleon's Travelling Bookshelf

'Quite, quite,' thought Too-ticky with a little sigh. 'It's always like this in their adventures. To save and be saved. I wish somebody would write a story sometime about the people who warm up the heroes afterwards.'

Moominland Midwinter, Tove Jansson

Wild Boar of New York

Remembering how Aristotle felt
metal-bound and hard to the throat,

the swart boar flirts the stoop.
Snaffling for trash, his ridgeback wig

stands stiff as a disguise.
He bides his time.

Haunted by the cuff of his feet
in sweet grass,

the burst flute of Aphrodite's calls
as he put her young god to the gore.

The Boy Who Read Homer to His Cat

Hengist the family cat is dying.
His blue-stone paws pulled tight
beneath his chin, he has taken notes

on the benefits of mewling,
decided quietly, now, he shall abstain.
Over his head you breathe

hot deities; the warm,
narrative assurances of Sleep
and Dream. But in his language

light does not seep beneath doorways;
it heaves from shouldered torches
across the broken fields at dawn.

He thinks about the hardening of earth
about a barrow. The point
at which his eyes will narrow

to the split-width of a star
and he shall raise his rift of fur
against the northern winds,

his soul flying out over the whale-road,
unfettered by these wordy consolations
of wandering and return.

Napoleon's Travelling Bookshelf

They'll see you've gone,
then starve in what you burned.

Snow's slow elegy, over bone,
rings through throats of glass.

Longing for the language of furs
they pick their way

through the blackened brackets of home,
the places

where hot remarks left signals in the air
and where now

they must string up sparrows for meat,
praying for the white-winged duke to appear.

In your carriage,
cloaked in the folds of empire,

notes scratch their way into your copybook:
'coconut milk, a Pyrrhic dance, Timandra'.

The combative crack of a Russian frost
thrills books as you cast them to the ground.

Coney Island Cribs

The Electric Michaelangelo's
given up carving arms next door.

The haruspicator's entrails
have boiled themselves to soup.

If you want to find Captain Bonavita
when he's done

repeating early Baudelaire
to his lions,

then sneak past the generator's burr
and take a peek

at these faces pulled from waists too soon,
these improbable fruits

whose stuttered mewlings
have got the Fat Lady sitting

and knitting snug booties,
prompted Lobster Boy

and the Invisible Man
to spend less time than they might

over chess. A million lightbulbs
hum loosely around the boardwalk fence.

They taunt the moon. Her blank particulars
shunt the tide in protest.

Genova

For Emily

February,

and you are bathing in pearls
while I abandon newspaper
to the fierce, floored kisses of marble.

The light sees right through me here
- and the smile of your new lover's leaving.
From above

the morning laundry sniffs and drips,
as when an aged aunt comes calling.
It is little more

than an ache in the weather.
An envelope from home
which shall lie unopened

for several hours, or more.

Tulips

She has married the mouths of her tulips
with string. Five intermittent stitches loop
each gentle petal to the listing rim.
The light is all wrong for this time of year,
and the quiet fear that the blooms won't hold
assails her while she's drinking tea.
How difficult can it be for them
to hold their wealth until the wedding's here,
until her daughter's soft, untutored
hand, slips inside hers, confides her fear.
They'll slice each spilling thread together,
a mother's love, from an exploding cup.
In the garage a pile of wooden spools,
and a sewing box lid, that's tightly shut.

The Ladies of France Buy New Shoes

They will not do anymore, these pre-war heels;
with their yawning tips, their hummingbird beak
that shook hips on uneven keels.

It is our backs straightening up from the field
that say: this is how we will arc for you;
in the press of a hand upon a spade we've come to feel

a husband's hand, that's waiting for his dues.
Old shoes hide in the cupboard, small relics
of lives scribbled in a careless font.

We take hot-paced strides along the street,
the whole foot leaving the ground at once.

Lillith's Lament

Still pinned to his myth of innocence.

Though by the time she had slipped
beneath his planetary ribs, he and I
had already been gods in the mud.

Still reigned up to creation.
But whilst she felt the world's fast stamp
in her womb, I had sunk my feet in oceans.

They carved my name on amulets;
I stalked the earth through mirrors, then became
the *Night Jar* where a scorpion slept

between my legs, a goddess
with the dripping feet of a screech owl
and the deafening wings of *Karina, Lamashtu*.

I taught my children several things:
never to roost where the apples grow;
never consent to lying below.

Saturday Night Fly

Tag: gold twist and light blue silk

Tail: small topping with Indian crow

Butt: a spreading of Mandarin drake

Body: black floss, this should be sparely laid on

Ribs: silver tinsel, very narrow, seven turns

Hackle: blue, from yellow seal's fur

Wings: double jungle, red macaw and feathered cock

Cheeks: fat chatterer

Head: black herl

Brazen irons: No 5, to suit the field

'An excellent killer....'

Iris

Because she can wear flowers or daub herself
in the dulling blood of cattle, or screw
her face into wooden play-shapes;
she can shroud each limb with lace from a veil
of the most retiring virgin, or fade
away all the rainbows with a harlot's rouge;
and still no man will paint her.

And only a blue winged beetle-casing
catches the meanest wink of her hair,
brighter than ink, an oily spot
powerless to drown itself in water.

The Ballroom at West Riding Asylum

The frail compass of her head
has led her here.

Six pieces of the alphabet elude her
but still,

she's learnt the value of stripping
the orange fruit from its rind,

that not every square-framed window
is a landscape painting, disguised.

It seems polite to mention when she's feeling
more than unusually small.

And now this new necessity
of forever remembering the waltz.

Bonfire Night in the Old People's Home

Such bangs about the heart!
The dark silhouette of each china horse
seems to stamp a military pirouette.

Here is a laughing shadow puppet
with a stick. Here the play of oily lights
over glass stopped eyes.

Maria in room fifty-four can suddenly
recall that petunia
was always her colour.

Lit from behind by boxed stars,
a network of gummy smiles unravels
at the night's fast, exorbitant fizz.

July

A month
of leaping trout.
The villagers dusted earth from their boots,
muttered of meanings caught lurking in the corn.

It befits such tales to begin with a stranger.
And so she seemed: the pots unwashed,
the blackberries gone to rot inside the door.
Nights were worse.

I am thrice blessed by moonlight, he declared,
and she kissed his scars in brazen view
of that common nunnery gossip.

Later, when the cows wouldn't calve,
and her neighbour held a barrel
to the head of his hound, she would testify, only

to this: that his night-rushed skin
turned to smoke come the morning.
And the rising light across sky-rocked fields,
came like a command from home.

The Poet Takes a Walk on Deck

Then I'll turn this barrel over,
sluice the night through and suffer
these grim little fish to expire.

Eels whelp at stars,
and it is far too late to go imagining,
or to throw a line out to some
considerable city
where we might take pleasure
in a guttural arch.

We could enquire as to the health
of plumblines, I suppose,
slip knots round the thoughts of sailors,
whose shantied breaths blow holes in sleep.

They scrape new names into their arms.
All our black inks long for land.

Faking

Though you have not yet
thrown my world out to that depth
where the finspines scut
and giggle across
the surface of their darkened nets -
I do not love you any less.
I am content to form
the small oh, of glory,
to add a little polish
to your morning epaulettes.

It is much, I imagine,
as the mouths of those
court whores who flung
their broken praises
round mock-epic beds.
(A strumpfhosen cover
for the dependable teapot;
a slice of mutton
when the evening's spent).

The dissolution of the bones of St Cuthbert

                        is quick.
Performed by the priest in the shadows,
behind the shriek of the holly bush.

The butcher, clutching at a thighbone,
decides he shall string it like a purple ham.

The trapper, intrigued by the spaces in the face,
promises to flesh it again, with skins.

Everyone distrusts the blacksmith.

'But my time-smudged forge is perfect,' he declares
for vanishing a bright, white thing.

Only the farmer suggests a respectable burial -
a grave dug in the slog of a plough,

and the local fool, he'll wrap it in his innocence,
wave it like a rattle in the town.

Daughters of Elmet

Cut from the fading swatch of weaving stock;
to come home is to be reminded

that women have not done well here:
the three sisters and their tinderbox of stories,

the poet with a high dark cry in her ear
whose stone pokes out of the February snow

no higher than a muddied bootscrape.
The moor lifts the scruffed hem of her skirt

to those who might try and heel her.
She strikes the cobbles in high-laced boots;

let's find the skeletons, she whispers
in a drenched circle of leaves.

'I Have a Young Sister'

after the Middle English

I have a soft-eyed sister
        Strays far beyond the sea,
And many are the remembrances
        That she has yielded me.

She sent me a blistered cherry
        Sighing, empty of its stone
And a pale-flecked crystal dove that slept
        And held no thrusting bones.

She sent me a fresh pulled briar
        White, set loose from thornpiked skin
And urged me to clutch my darling but beware
        The dark pressed nights of longing.

But then how is the cherry sweet you say
        If spilled without its stone?
And how could any pure plumed dove
        Be left to die alone?

How could the creeping briar pluck
        Without its piercing skin?
How might I sway my sweetheart close
        beyond the fatal hand of longing?

When the cherry still sang the flower's hopes
        Then it hadn't any stone
When the dove was a warm pressed egg it slept

Without the stick of bone.

The briar's sweet and sleeping seed
  Was free of thorny skin,
When my girl takes hold at that point of want
  She outstrips the ties of longing.

Green Song

pick any green   grass-green   emerald   verdigris
asparagus   pine   green-eyed glass
pick snake   or spinach   or village-green
absinthe   olive   fresh tarragon   moss
a pea-green boat   a wicked queen
oscar wilde's carnations   camouflage   green tea
a dollar bill   mint   a gooseberry fool
a green-eyed monster   a woodland pool
pick jade   or copper   or fig   or lime
fecundity   hope   a shamrock   a vine
pick spring   green-leaf shadows   a glade   thick ivy
pick eden   the light   unsure of itself

Two Views of the Crystal Palace Dinosaurs

Dinner inside the Iguanadon
New Year's Eve, 1853

Releasing the meat from the bones came easy;
the barrel of the goose like a Christmas bell,
the tinsel string - a stand-in for the spine -
dips weakly now towards the crystal and the din.

Each guest has pleased his opposite.
The duet of soup, the jugged hare;
and what else then might a skeleton be for,
if not to make an upright man of him?

I'll tell you what's beastly! they roar,
as the claret removes his name and his skin.
Midnight sounds like a pulse in the skull.
Nothing he wants is shocking.

Dinosaur bathtime
Crystal Palace, 1930

Washing the eye of the Ichthyosaur takes time:

the cold bucket cleaving to the hands like ash,
the difficult reach on a long-handled broom.

They shake the fog from their coats and begin
to scrub at the abiding jibes of grass,

the lives of flowers, mute incursions of moss
pressed deep into crannies of bone.

His body brings silence to the park like snow.

A grim image of teeth below the water
to the right of the sign that reads 'No Boating.'

The Tattooed Rose Gardener

Like kittens complaining their claws
he says,   or the sinister smiles
of insects.   Either way,
needles don't spit   the same stories
as thorns.   Their hearts are ruder,
but the shoulder is a better place,
and all those   hard won princesses,
asleep for years   under the glass,
might wish they'd pricked
simpler names   into their arms.
Keep a wolf   on your back
and your back   to the door,
lust   bragging on the bone.

Waiting for the Indiana Night Moth

Citheronia Royalis or King of the Poets

From beneath the staggered repeats of a quilt
stitched by the ladies of the Monroe County fair,

we watch a ribbon of lizard cast his tongue about
for meat, consider the care with which

a spiny janitor uncurls his face into the grass.
The firebugs are dancing their delicious polka;

the chrysanthemums, fat copper bells, tempt us to strike
feathered notes into the air; across the street

a dog hollers and his black correspondences
settle on the neighbourhood like ash.

Benjamin smokes a cigarette. His first,
he says, since reading Henry James,

and like a fire-eater, with his throat thrown back
he yawns small smoke rings. We light a candle

expecting the mutter of wings, our stoop a star
to draw the king, a flurry of blurry white sounds.

And we tell ourselves that there are nights
when the court may call for a wonder.

Garden

Time often arrives late these days.
A muscle exhausted by arrangement,
a tremulous leg that sinks
into the wicker of an ageing chair.

I have much need of the garden.
Below the sunken lips of the wall
there is a place, where the bellies of birds
can soar above us, strange moons.

But then I fear you are no true navigator.
The fish hooks, the star book and the seeds
teased whatever it was ran scutting
through your shed last night.
And at my age it does not do
to see fright on the faces of flowerpots.

The irises are so very blue this year,
though the gnarled habits of their beds were black.
The clods of winter soil burnt strangely,
incorrigible to the spade.

Afternoons at *Same Fusy*

Even the black cat knows me here.
Her slender frame insists
it is my leg inside the door.

The grape-stained lamps are still hung too low.

Here, is where we would take tea
with the mathematicians, suffer
the rapier beards of revolution to sigh,
It is always too cold to speak of Moscow.

Such was the comfort in knowing
the dear little elbows of the diplomat's wife.
And oh, the difference,
in those who removed their hats hopefully,
detaching the snow-spun streets from the sky.

We had deserved such things
as would bring about a gasp,
cousin to the snappish intoxication of ice.
The wind on widening avenues
should have shattered blossomed fruit
to the ground.

There is no mentioning the doctor anymore.

The quiet intervention of an extra chair
reflects in the brassy counter bell.

Warsaw Uprising

This is the brack and the flail,
of mudsuck and sewer-snipe.

Of nights, spent fully clothed in Babcia's arms,
of torchlight and broken hair dreams.

Jakub is scrying a horse onto slate.

He says it brings him peace to imagine
its damp nostrils distended, wide to the air,
the cold clamming sweat of its back.

We are all holed up in the cellars of our skulls.

Trying to ignore the dropped letters everywhere,
that there's no one left to utter *czjuwaj*, or run
this shivering glut of pipes.

Even our vocabulary is wounded,
save the words 'fire', 'stone' and 'boot'.

In monuments the flat of our eyes
is dull beneath green cascades of water.

The Ravensbrück Seamstress

She bites buttons from the coats of dead men.
Fillets the seams of grain sacks for thread.
Spits when repairing the outline of stars.

Mud is murder on the hems. They come to her
for pockets that might save a photograph, a ring.
Cuffs are fashionably frayed that year. Waists cinched in.

When Reuben dies by the train track, in the rain,
twelve girls are wearing his socks by lunch.
Each thick red stitch she forces through their collars

irritates the skin, reminds them to struggle.
They break ice for mirrors for a treat when it's cold,
worn faces, suddenly respectable to themselves.

The year is 2095 and Bjorn is planting seeds from the Norwegian Ark

When he dreams he sees a vast untended field.

Poppies cheering their exultant widow's weeds,

the shudder of unkempt cherries where they hung

by the flatstone wall, where the blackbird sung.

Anything save these seeds that are nothing

but a roughening dust on the tongue.

Thin children kept hidden in a cupboard

who have waited for a little air, the morning sun.

23 Kinds of Solitaire

According to Edmund Hoyle there are twenty-three different kinds of
solitaire, more than all other card games together.
Doris Grumbach, *Fifty Days of Solitude*

American Toad   squats in the mist   a mouthful of chamber music
Betsy Ross   often remembers   her first five-pointed star

Captive Queens   ransomed in battle   commemorate heroes in
                                     twists of hair
Der Kleine Napoleon   victim in Paris   a fine example   of the
                                     cruellest cut

Everest   the climb on the steep side they say   is something akin
                                     to scaling paper walls
Fascination Fan   with great tails   they scatterbrag dust and
                                     rainbows

Glencoe   a white and blinded root   still pushes at the bones of
                                     horses
Hit or Miss   the knifethrower   can't help but love his girl

Interregnum   it's a quiet   period   for hats
Jacqueline   opts   for the oversized sunglasses

Kerosene   hell   is a red skinned balloon
Lido of Venice   the stones incredulous   watery feet   on a sudden
                                     path

Miss Milligan   diddles her feet to time   turns to and carries on
Norway   the winter refastens itself   trees forgetting themselves

in snow

Odessa   the guns sunk under the ice   angels retreating   from a
woeful steel
Peonies   with their loaded hearts   like to be left alone

Quartets   the fourth book   puts a stop to adventure
Rainfall   a sweet   interrogation of the land

Shanghai   rots in the dirty air   a spire of sin   curls slowly up
wards
Two rings   softly loosen   on the day of dying

Waning Moon   the working out   is threatened by the jaw of
eclipse
Yukon Double Rail   singing   down the line

Zodiac   the problem   of twelve shadows   all anxiously rising to
meet you

Rainy Day in the Drawing Room

All the weapons of December are here:
the lowered knife of the sky, my sister's
fingers like a herd of horses
        are retreating across the piano.

Some silkened box for the heart, please.
Some room where there's no clock and we
can make play with the unfinished children
        whose names are whispered near bedroom locks.

The lake is frozen again, they say.
The grey anvil beak of mama's favourite bird
        keeps dashing against the cage.

The Theft of Sybille of Cleves

Because an unrepeatable life
might always have been enough.

Just as that irrelevant key in the pot
still remembers what caused the creak

behind doors, so this gentle waiter's bride
knew how her husband wound the clock,

she would always have wept
of his death to his heirs: that old man

who stood up too quick and sat down
again by the *rue du Campile* tram stop.

There was no need for his midnight fingers
on the frame. That cold walk home

from the closed museum. His name
forgotten, but his story made.

The Funeral

A room of borrowed black thrums:
the vexed hush in the small-boned breath of starlings
preparing to flee the field.

We are too young for this,
and unlike your crab-stride hand
pushed up my skirt, or that
regrettable nip of gin,
this morning it would appear to matter.

Each current heart drums loudly
as if to rouse the colours free from their lead,
as if to say, so now it is
we might begin to believe
that we are really here.

Tonight, we shall travel home on bicycles,
your shirt-flaps sprung, evasive and loose
in the dark dizzying fingers of the wind.

Casting

The kingdom in her corset fold;
let me never play that queen, who,
heavy-lidded in her affairs of state,
boils jewels for dinner,
sips from the hearts of princes
caught faltering at centre-stage.

Much rather, the messenger
who will take the letter
that is always delivered too late.
Slipping scenes somewhere on the ship
to Norway. Lost from sight
behind the ice-mapped waves.

Chaconne for Ice

after Robert Francis

1
Fierce coupling
of fever and bite: the icicle.

2
Flawless
the endlessly falling flakes.

3
I freeze
therefore I am.

4
Unmelting dead
please put down your hands.

5
1912
A remembrance of deck quoits.

6
Amundsen drives
five dogs to their death.

7
Small boy with mirror in your eye,
why can't you spell eternity?

8
A poem dreamt.
Cold clear perfection.

9
Always winter
and never Christmas?

10
Scintillating blade
mark my single figure's grace.

11
'Love on the rocks'
slow bar stool entropy.

12
(Please whisper when speaking
the avalanche's name.)

13
freddo how else
Bentley's barefoot violin?

14
Cold fractals
multiplications in the dark

15
Ultima thule
white limits of our reach.

Suzanna Ibsen is cold

She does not forgive him these November days.
Insidious snow; the slow burning

of drama in the blue-black stove. Ghosts
live in her bones. She knows

they're opening doors in search
of palazzos, each dull creak of her joints

the rack of disappointment. Brickwork astonishes her.
And there is no escaping his command

of the house: his large theatre-throat
berating the portraits, stone devils

hiding in his fingertips. When he is gone
her solace is the upright chair. She thinks

it will make it easier for her
to see him, giving out the sun.

NOTES

'Wild Boar of New York'
The apple now traditionally served in the mouth of a boar is thought to originate in the actions of an enterprising young Oxford scholar, who defended himself against a charging boar in the forest of Shotover by thrusting a metal-covered copy of Aristotle into the creature's jaws.

'The Boy Who Read Homer to His Cat'
Hengest or Hengist is the name of a semi-legendary ruler of Kent in the fifth century, allegedly the first Saxon king of England.

'Napoleon's Travelling Bookshelf'
White sparrows were known as 'dukes' in Tsarist Russia, and were believed to have the power to grant wishes.

'Lillith's Lament'
There are hundreds of legends in different traditions pertaining to the demon Lillith. In Christianity she appears as Adam's disobedient first wife.

'Two Views of the Crystal Palace Dinosaurs'
A woodcut showing Benjamin Waterhouse Hawkins' banquet inside the cast of an iguanodon can be viewed online by typing 'crystal palace dinosaurs' into Wikipedia.

'Daughters of Elmet'
Elmet covered a broad area in what is now the West Riding of Yorkshire.

'Warsaw Uprising'

Czuwaj or 'be ready' was the motto of Polish scouts who ran a resistance postal service through the sewers of Warsaw during the German occupation of the 1940s.

'23 Kinds of Solitaire'

Despite Edmund Hoyle's assertion, Wikipedia lists over a hundred different names for the card game. Some of the names used here are drawn from that list. Others are purely fictional.

'Chaconne for Ice'

Wilson Alwyn "Snowflake" Bentley pioneered the photographing of snowflakes. Apparently, he was also sometimes to be seen playing his violin barefoot in the snow.

'Suzanna Ibsen is Cold'

Suzanna Ibsen, wife of the celebrated playwright, outlived her husband by eight years. She refused to die in bed, spending each day during her final illness sat on a hard-backed kitchen chair.